BRAVE BALLERINA

The Story of
Janet Collins

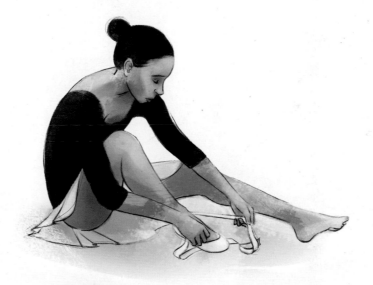

MICHELLE MEADOWS

illustrated by EBONY GLENN

HENRY HOLT AND COMPANY
NEW YORK

This is the girl
who danced in the breeze
to the *swoosh, swoosh, swoosh*
of towering trees.

These are the costumes
her dear mama made.
Costumes for lessons—
that's how they paid.

These are the pointe shoes,
shiny and pink,
small, quick steps—
plink, plink, plink.

This is the audience,
lined up in rows,
cheering her on as
she danced on her toes.

This is the family
that lifted her high,
supporting her dreams
right up to the sky.

This is the backbend,

low to the ground,

which she practiced until
it was perfectly round.

This is the trio,
Three Shades of Brown—
daredevil dancers,
the talk of the town.

This is the time,
way back in the day,
when dance schools turned
black students away.

This is the teacher
who stood by her side.
Knees bending deep
and arms open wide.

THE AUDIT

LOS ANGELES

BALLET RUSSE DE MON
TONIGHT ONLY "GIS
DOORS OPEN 6:00 PM

35

This is the streetcar
she rode in the dark,

to see ballerinas
making their mark.

This is the dancer
who found her way in,
but learned she would
have to lighten her skin.

This is the girl
with a broken heart.
But she bounced right back
and made a new start.

This is the dancer
who kept going strong,
bare feet flying
to a Spanish song.

This is the music—
bum, bum, bum.
Back and forth to
the beat of a drum.

This is the class,
a welcoming place,
that focused on talent
regardless of race.

This is the sweat
that dripped from her skin

when she practiced alone,
again and again.

This is the dancer
who went back for more

when her tender toes ached
and her muscles felt sore.

This is the body,
expressions so real.
Gestures and movements
that made people feel.

This is the man
who saw her perform
and knew she would take
the world by storm.

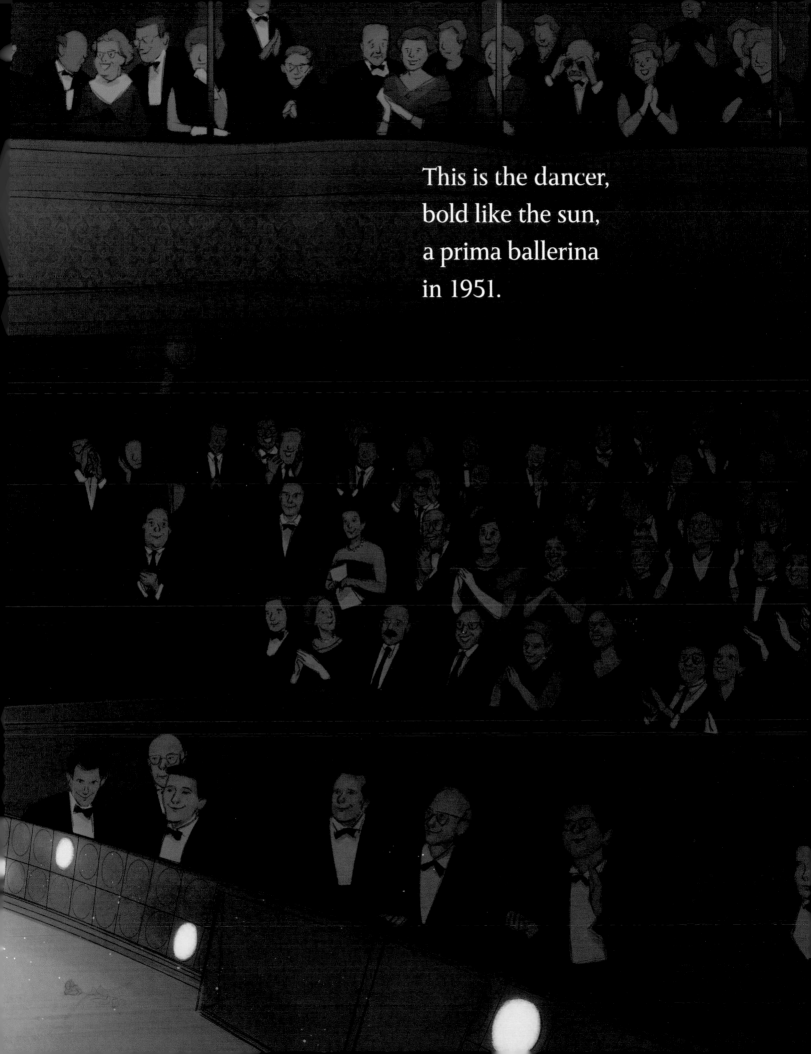

This is the dancer,
bold like the sun,
a prima ballerina
in 1951.

AUTHOR'S NOTE

Janet Collins in 1951, the year she first performed at the Metropolitan Opera House

As a young child, I took ballet at the Jones-Haywood Dance School in Washington, DC, which was founded in 1941 to give African American children a chance to study ballet at a time when opportunities were limited. I loved getting dressed up in costume and performing in recitals. Many years later when my son went off to college, I began taking ballet as an adult. This experience brought back fond memories of my mother taking me to ballet lessons on Saturday mornings. It also led me on a path of researching black ballerinas and ultimately discovering the amazing life of Janet Collins. I set out to write a lyrical tribute to Janet's life.

What I love about Janet's story is that nothing could keep her from dancing. Janet was dancing at a time when segregation, the separation of racial groups, was common in the United States. She was born in New Orleans, Louisiana, in 1917. She moved with her family to Los Angeles, California, around the age of four. Her father was a tailor and her mother was a seamstress. To pay for Janet's dance lessons, her mother made costumes for recitals. Janet's family believed in her abilities and rooted for her to succeed. When she couldn't enroll in a ballet school because of discrimination, Janet sought private lessons.

As a teenager, Janet auditioned for the Ballet Russe de Monte Carlo. Her talent was evident, but she was told that she could only join the Ballet Russe on the condition that she paint her skin white in order to blend in with the other dancers onstage. She said no, walked away from the company, cried . . . and kept on dancing. Because of her talent and perseverance, she landed in classes with many amazing teachers, including Carmelita Maracci, who blended ballet with Spanish dance and held integrated ballet classes. Janet also studied modern dance with Lester Horton and Katherine Dunham, who developed a unique combination of ballet, Caribbean dance, and African dance.

Janet Collins holds a flower bouquet in her dressing room after performing at the Met Opera on November 13, 1951.

A man named Zachary Solov, who was ballet master at the Metropolitan Opera House, saw Janet perform and was blown away. He arranged for her to be hired by the general manager, Rudolf Bing. Janet is best known for becoming the first African American prima ballerina with the Metropolitan Opera House in 1951, but she was a versatile, award-winning performer who also excelled at modern and ethnic dance. She had many talents; she was a painter, choreographer, and teacher, and was devoted to helping others.

Janet's presence in the dance world has often been described as a dazzling, captivating light—a light that blazed a trail for aspiring dancers everywhere. Janet died in 2003 at the age of eighty-six.

SOURCES

Ballet Russes, documentary film, Zeitgeist Films, 2005.

Black Ballerina, documentary film, Shirley Road Productions, 2015.

"Blacks in Ballet," documentary video clip, *I'll Make Me a World*, PBS, 1999.

Dancing in the Light: The Janet Collins Story, animated film, Sweet Blackberry Productions, 2015.

De Lavallade, Carmen. "The Dancer Who Made History 64 Years Before Misty Copeland." *Time* magazine, July 13, 2015.

Dunning, Jennifer. "Janet Collins, 86." *The New York Times*, May 31, 2003.

"Janet Collins: To Dance Is to Live," documentary video clip, M. J. Washington, 2009.

Lewin, Yäel. "Janet Collins: A Spirit That Knows No Bounds." *Dance Magazine*, February 1997.

Lewin, Yäel Tamar. *Night's Dancer: The Life of Janet Collins: With Her Unfinished Autobiography.* Middletown, CT: Wesleyan University Press, 2011.

Lille, Dawn. "Katherine Dunham: Dancer, Choreographer, Educator, Activist and Innovator." *Dance Magazine*, November 2010.

Ramirez, Marc. "The Blazing Steps of Janet Collins." *The Seattle Times*, January 23, 2000.

Straus, Rachel. "Technique: The Hows of Horton." *Dance Magazine*, January 2010.

Vaughan, David. "Janet Collins: The First African-American Artist Under Regular Contract at the Met." *The Guardian*, June 10, 2003.

WEBSITES

New York Public Library for the Performing Arts
nypl.org/locations/lpa

Prima: The Janet Collins Story
primajanetcollins.com

International Association of Blacks in Dance
iabdassociation.org

For dancer and choreographer Tikiri Shapiro,
and for Amy Miyoshi and Lori Smyth
—M. M.

For all who dare to make their dreams a reality,
and in memory of the talented Janet Collins
—E. G.

Henry Holt and Company, *Publishers since 1866*
Henry Holt® is a registered trademark of Macmillan Publishing Group, LLC
175 Fifth Avenue, New York, NY 10010 • mackids.com

Text copyright © 2019 by Michelle Meadows
Illustrations copyright © 2019 by Ebony Glenn
All rights reserved.

Library of Congress Cataloging-in-Publication Data is available.
Names: Meadows, Michelle.
Title: Brave ballerina : the story of Janet Collins / Michelle Meadows ; illustrated by Ebony Glenn.
Description: New York : Henry Holt and Company, [2019]
Identifiers: LCCN 2018020972 | ISBN 978-1-250-12773-0 (hardcover)
Subjects: LCSH: Collins, Janet, 1917–2003. | Ballet dancers—United
States—Biography. | Ballerinas—United States—Biography. | African American dancers—Biography.
Classification: LCC GV1785.C634 M43 2019 | DDC 792.802/8092 [B] —dc23
LC record available at https://lccn.loc.gov/2018020972

Our books may be purchased in bulk for promotional, educational, or business use.
Please contact your local bookseller or the Macmillan Corporate and Premium Sales Department at
(800) 221-7945 ext. 5442 or by e-mail at MacmillanSpecialMarkets@macmillan.com.

First edition, 2019 / Designed by Patrick Collins
The artist used Adobe Photoshop to create the art for this book.
Printed in China by Hung Hing Off-set Printing Co. Ltd., Heshan City, Guangdong Province

1 3 5 7 9 10 8 6 4 2